Five Steps to Avoid the School-to-Prison Pipeline

QUISHA & OMAR BROWN

Access PowerPoint Presentations and other support materials for this workbook at: **www.YouthWorkbook.com**

DEDICATION

This workbook is dedicated to our children Brandon (age 17), Nathan (age 5) and Mayah (3 months old). We hope that this workbook will be used to help improve the outcomes for minority male and female youth; thereby decreasing the number of youth becoming trapped in the school to prison pipeline.

"God, grant me the serenity to accept the things I cannot change; courage to change the things I can; and wisdom to know the difference."~Reinhold Niebuhr (1892-1971)

Table of Contents

Introduction

Purpose of this workbook.
This workbook is uniquely formatted to be used as a discussion tool to encourage logical thinking and improved decision making for middle to high school students and their families using a Restorative Practice Circle discussion setting. Teens, parents and educators are encouraged to participate in the Restorative Circle using this workbook with youth whenever possible. For more information on Restorative Circles, please visit http://www.iirp.edu/.

What is a Restorative Practice Circle?
According to the International Institute for Restorative Practices (IIRP), "Restorative Practices, which evolved from restorative justice, is a new field of study that has the potential to positively influence human behavior and strengthen civil society around the world. Restorative practices build healthy communities, increases social capital, reduces the impact of crime, decreases antisocial behavior, repairs harm and restores relationships."

Restorative Circles provide a practical forum for the resolution of underlying feelings that intrude into the classroom and disrupt learning. Underlying feelings may stem from the home, school or community environment.

What is the school to prison pipeline?
The school to prison pipeline can be described as a series of events that move you straight from the classroom to prison. Events could include the causes (i.e. unauthorized cell phone usage, etc) that lead to students constantly being suspended or skipping school. As a result of not being in school, these students tend to be at a higher risk of becoming involved in more dangerous and risky activity while not in school.

Why is it important to make good decisions as a minority youth?
A recent report from the National Council on Crime & Delinquency found that Black and Hispanic youth are treated much worse than white youth once they enter the criminal juvenile system even when they are charged with the same crime. The reality is that as a youth, you have very little control over this kind of unequal treatment. One thing that you do have control over are the choices you make.

How can this workbook help?
This workbook uses real life situations that students can relate to. Many of the stories in this book come from real life events witnessed or experienced by the Authors.

Each step discussed in this workbook uses real life scenarios from the lives of fictional characters Jaleesa, Robert, their parents and friends. Each scenario and discussion is followed by a set of questions to stimulate thinking around better decision making. The scenario and questions call for frequent pausing to allow time for reflection and discussion. Youth, parents and educators are able to understand problems and issues from various viewpoints and not just their own.

Meet Mom & Dad

Meet Jaleesa

Meet Robert

Step 1: Become more involved in your own education
"It is easier to build strong children than to repair broken men." —Frederick Douglass

You will be an adult very soon and there is no better time to start taking more responsibility for your own education than right now. It is never too late to start learning, but the earlier you start, the easier it will be for you in college.

Just like your body needs food for you to have energy and grow, your brain also needs food to learn and grow. Education is like food for your brain. It is for this reason that you will see the term "Food for thought" used a lot in this workbook. The questions asked are purposely designed to stimulate your brain to think hard about various situations, not just from your own point of view, but from other people's (i.e. teachers, parents, etc) point of view as well.

Getting suspended is not cool

Your ability to get a good education is negatively impacted if you're not in school to receive it.

We would like to introduce you to Jaleesa, a smart but very sassy young lady in the 9th grade. Jaleesa is suspended at least once a month. Most of the time, she gets in trouble for her unauthorized cell phone usage during class time. Her school has a zero-tolerance policy, so there are really no other options of discipline for students at her school. Her school does claim to use Restorative Circles[1], however, the use of this strategy is not fully enforced at her school.

Let's read more about what happened to Jaleesa during class and then we will answer a few questions.

Jaleesa's Cell Phone

"Jaleesa please stop talking and distracting the other students from learning," demands Ms. Smith. "If you don't want to do the work, then just leave so that those that want to learn, can learn," Ms. Smith continued in a stern voice.

"Nobody's learning anything," Jaleesa replied sarcastically. "Who can learn from these boring worksheets that you give us every day, they don't even make sense. Why don't you get up from your desk and teach us something like you are supposed to, then maybe I'll sit down and listen," Jaleesa added.

Suddenly, Jaleesa got an amazing idea. She wanted to take a picture of Ms. Smith sitting at her desk, doing absolutely nothing but surfing the internet and post it online. Jaleesa reached in her pocket and pulled out her cell phone, then took a picture of Ms. Smith.

"Jaleesa! Give me the cell phone, right now! I did not give you permission to take my picture," shouted a very upset Ms. Smith.

---

[1] Restorative Circles provide a practical forum for the resolution of underlying feelings that intrude into the classroom and disrupt learning.

Jaleesa refused to give Ms. Smith her cell phone. After taking the picture, Jaleesa placed the phone back in her pocket.

"I didn't even take your picture," Jaleesa lied to Ms. Smith as she turned to smile at her classmates.

Ms. Smith called security. Security rushed to the room. Ms Smith explained to security what happened. Jaleesa tried to interrupt and explain her side, but she was interrupted by security.

"You know the rules, but you keep wanting to do what you want to do. Let's go right now," said the security guard in a very mean and frustrated tone.

Jaleesa has clearly violated the school's insubordination and cell phone policy. First, taking a picture of someone without their permission is against the law and school policy. Secondly, cell phone usage during class, without teacher permission, is a direct violation of school policy as well.

Consequently, Jaleesa is immediately taken to the office by security and suspended for 3 days.

Food for thought:

In this story, do you believe that immediate suspension was a fair punishment? Why or why not? If not, what in your opinion would have been a fairer consequence?

_____
_____
_____

Do you believe Jaleesa or the teacher could have done anything differently in this situation that could have prevented Jaleesa from being suspended? If yes, what?

_____
_____
_____

There are always two sides to every story. Let us now take a look at the day Jaleesa got suspended from Ms. Smith point of view.

Ms. Smith's Efforts

Ms. Smith's first hour class is coming in the classroom now, taking their sweet time, talking loudly, cursing and horse playing around as usual. Ms. Smith is trying to hurry them in so that she can lock the door behind the last person as soon as the bell rings. The rules are that if a student is late, they should not be allowed into class. Teachers like this rule because it is a great way to help students develop a sense of urgency about being on time and it also helps to keep out students known to cause the most trouble during class.

"Everyone, please come in, sit down and pull out paper and pen for bell work. You all know the routine." Ms. Smith yells as she does every day, at least six times a day for each new class hour. She must yell because there is so much noise in the classroom that she can barely hear herself when she is yelling.

"Anthony, Charles, Myra, Jaleesa, put away your cell phones or get them taken!

Thomas, please stop using all of that profanity in my classroom.

Michael leave Brittany alone and go to your own seat.

Samantha, get your feet off the table.

Excuse me young man, who are you and what class do you belong in? Please get out of my class before I call security!

Michele please put the mirror away, this is not a beauty contest.

Everyone, please, please, please settle down, we have a lot to cover today in preparation for the state test that is coming in a couple weeks. I need you to sit down and complete your bell work, so that we can review it. Students, please listen to me. Students!" Ms. Smith repeats tirelessly with a now crackling and tired voice.

Ms. Smith begins to sweat profusely, her heart beating a mile a minute. She can feel her blood pressure rising again.

"No one seems to be listening to me. Am I invisible? Do any of these students really care about life after high school?" she thought to herself.

"I' can't let this job kill me. I'd be better off just letting them do what they want and go sit at my desk to look for a new job on the computer. Going through this everyday is becoming much too stressful and my health is starting to suffer because of it." Ms. Smith continues to think to herself, drops her hands and walks back over to her desk to sit at the computer.

Ms. Smith notices Jaleesa walking toward her and sees a flash coming from Jaleesa's cell phone.

"Jaleesa! Give me the cell phone, right now! I did not give you permission to take my picture," shouts a very upset Ms. Smith.

Ms. Smith picks up the classroom phone to call security and they come to the room immediately.

"Security, I want that young lady suspended, she has a picture of me in her phone. I did not give her permission to take my picture. I asked her to give me the phone and she refused."

Food for thought:

There are many teachers like Ms. Smith who start out with the greatest enthusiasm to teach, only to have it slowly sucked away by students that don't want to cooperate. Imagine yourself as Ms. Smith in this situation.

How would you feel if you were Ms. Smith?

_____
_____

Do you think Ms. Smith is a bad or lazy teacher? Why or why not?

_____
_____

How would you handle behavior problems in this classroom if you were Ms. Smith?

_____
_____
_____

Now answer the same questions below that you answered earlier from Section 1. Pay special attention to whether or not your answers to these questions have now changed.

In the story about Jaleesa, do you believe that immediate suspension was a fair punishment? Why or why not?

_____
_____

Do you believe Jaleesa or the teacher could have done anything differently in this situation that could have prevented Jaleesa from being suspended? If yes, what?

_____
_____
_____

Did your answer change any to either of the previous questions? _____

If your answers changed, what do you believe caused your answer to change?

_____
_____

What are some of the most common reasons that students are suspended at your school?

_____
_____

Do you believe that suspension is the best form of punishment for the reasons you listed in the previous question? If no, explain.

_____

_____

_____

Jaleesa has been suspended so much that suspension just seems like a school vacation. Getting suspended a lot is causing her to lose valuable time that she could spend learning and preparing her brain for adult learning in college. Furthermore, it may also cause her to become involved in negative activities that she would not had become involved in if she were in school.

Have you ever been suspended or know someone who has? Think about how the time away from school was spent. What types of things did they or you do when not in school?

_____

_____

_____

Students who are suspended from school and already show some kind of behavioral problems or defiance to rules are clearly at a higher risk for getting into more trouble if they are not in school.

Suspending a student does not correct the bad behavior; it simply transfers the behavior to another environment, which is usually at home or in the streets. Youth who miss a lot of school due to excessive suspensions are generally more likely to become involved in physical fights, carry a weapon, smoke, use alcohol, marijuana and other drugs, and engage in sexual intercourse.

Do you believe that being suspended helps to make students feel bad or remorseful about what they have done? Why or why not?

_____

_____

_____

_____

Do you think excessive suspensions can lead to going to prison later in life? Why or why not?

_____

_____

Quick Tip

Avoiding school suspension:

How can you avoid being suspended from school? The solution is simple. Try your very best to follow your school's rules. Common rules to be aware of are those that involve the school's cell phone policy, insubordination, bullying, attendance policies and fighting.

Don't be a follower, instead be a leader.

No matter how much you may disagree with a specific rule, you must keep in mind that as a student your job is not to make the rules. Your job is to follow the rules. If you want to one day be the person who makes the rules, then you need to learn to follow them first.

Can you think of any other ways that you can avoid being suspended from school?

_____

_____

Out-dated books and technology

Many schools may struggle with getting the books and updated technology needed to best support learning in the 21st Century. Let's listen in on Ms. Smith's private discussion with Principal Duncan about the school's technology and textbooks.

Principal Duncan's Dilemma

"Good morning Mr. Duncan, the internet on the computers in the lab is moving very slow again today. It is very difficult for me to keep my students focused when we have to wait nearly 10 minutes for the page to load every time we click to move to the next sample test question. As a result, students have not been able to complete any of the practice tests to help them prepare for the online state assessments."

"Ms. Smith, thank you for bringing this to my attention. As the Principal, this definitely concerns me deeply. As you know, the District is having some very difficult financial troubles. Unfortunately, for now we must work with what we have until we can obtain some new computers or have these fixed. With that being said, please use the class textbooks and other resources that are in your classroom to help students prepare for the state assessments."

"With all due respect Sir, the textbooks that we have in the class now are from 1990, it is now 2016. The content that students are required to learn has changed tremendously since 1990. These books are much too old to help prepare my students for today's state required assessments."

Food for thought:

Is this the teacher or the Principal's fault for not keeping the newest books and technology? Of course not, the problem of old resources and technology often go beyond the Teacher's and many times the Principal's control. Without adequate resources to teach, it becomes very easy for teachers and students to get discouraged and lose their motivation to do what they are there to do, which is to teach or be taught.

Is there anything you believe that a student or Ms. Smith can do to help add to the classroom learning experience? Explain.

_____

_____

One example of what teachers or students can do to help add to classroom learning is given by Robert, Jaleesa's older brother. Robert is in the 10th grade.

Robert named his favorite and least favorite classes and then he explained why he chose each.

Robert's Favorite & Least Favorite Classes

My favorite class was my 7th grade Science class, taught by Mr. Vondrasek. He was a genuinely nice person and made learning fun. He would always ask us to help him research fun science activities online. I remember playing fun basketball games to help us learn science in that class. It made me feel really good too because I am the one that found the instructions for how to play game from searching online. I am in the 10th grade now and Science still happens to be my favorite subject because he made learning it so much fun.

My least favorite class was History, taught by Mrs. Schilbert in the 9th grade. She didn't seem to care much if we learned anything or not. Every day she would make us take notes the whole hour from PowerPoint slides that she found online somewhere. She didn't even understand the information on these PowerPoint slides herself. It was hard to learn in this class because she wasn't explaining the material. She was just reading what was on the PowerPoint slides.

Food for thought:

Learning can be so much fun when the environment is made to be fun and/or competitive in a non-threatening way. All students in the class should be given the same opportunity to win so that no one feels like they are at a disadvantage because they don't know the correct answers.

Engaging games like the basketball Science game are a perfect way to make any academic subject fun and more interesting. Everyone likes to have fun! Mr. Vondrasek also made a very wise choice by involving his students in helping to find the activity.

Have you ever found a cool educational classroom game/activity online that can be used in class? If yes, did you share it with anyone? Why or why not?

_____

_____

If you answered no to the question above, have you ever looked for an educational classroom game/activity online? Why or why not?

_____

_____

Do you feel like you should not have to look because you believe that this is the teacher's job and not yours? Why or why not?

_____

_____

_____

Why do you think Robert did not like Ms. Schilbert's class as much as Mr. Vondrasek's?

_____

_____

After learning about Mr. Vondrasek's class strategy from Robert, Ms. Smith had a bright idea for a way to engage her class in learning. Let's take a look at what happened when she introduced the idea to her class.

Ms. Smith's Bright Idea

"I'm feeling good! Today is a new day and I'm about to try out my new class game idea to help get my students get excited about learning U.S. History. I am super excited about this! If it worked for Mr. Vondrasek, then I am 100% positive it can work for my class too," Ms. Smith thought to herself as she set up the screen and projector to display the Jeopardy game that she had worked long hours on the night before.

"Good morning students! I have great news! Today, there will be no bell work! Instead, we are going to play a very fun game called JEOPARDY! I have a special prize for the winners. Everyone hurry now and gather in teams of 2 so we can get started."

Everyone looked excited and listened attentively to Ms. Smith as she went on to explain the rules.

"Alright now students, Let the games begin!" said Ms. Smith in an animated voice obviously designed to purposely ignite excitement.

Jaleesa asked, "Can I have Famous Presidents for 100 points?"

Ms. Smith replied, "Yes you can. Here is your clue: This is the name of the 4th President of the United States of America."

Jaleesa and her partner looked at one another with a puzzled look. It was obvious that neither of them knew the answer.

The room suddenly got very quiet. Ms. Smith asked, "Would any team like to try to guess the name? It does not necessarily have to be Jaleesa's team that gives the answer if they don't know it."

Jaleesa suddenly blurted out, "This game is stupid, who cares who the 4th President was? He is not the president anymore!" exclaimed a frustrated Jaleesa.

All of the other students in the class begin to laugh and agree with Jaleesa. The class immediately went back to talking loudly to one another and horse playing around as they tend to do every day in Ms. Smith's class.

Food for thought:

Why do you believe that Ms. Smith's attempt at using this game for her class did not go well?

_____

_____

Whose idea was it to play a Jeopardy game and who chose the questions for the game?

_____

Why do you believe Jaleesa got upset when she could not answer the question?

_____

_____

Why do you believe that the whole class lost interest in playing the game after Jaleesa's statement?

_____

_____

What suggestions would you have given to Ms. Smith that would have made the game more fun and engaging for the students?

_____

_____

_____

Do you feel like it is helpful for students to have some input when it comes to classroom learning activities? Why or why not?

_____

_____

As a student, you may not be the teacher, but your input about ways to help you learn best is very valuable. Most teachers are open to suggestions on how to best make learning fun and relevant for you.

Teachers look very good to their bosses when students in their classes succeed academically. When you succeed or improve academically, you look good to your parents, teachers and to potential colleges! Everyone likes to look good. Everyone wins when teachers and students are able to work together to determine creative ways to make learning fun and engaging.

If you need help finding suggestions for games/activities, Google is a really great place to start!

Quick Tip

Google has millions of classroom activities and learning tools! We did a Google search for "Teaching aids for high school science" and hundreds of results were returned. You could also type in "Teaching games or activities" and whatever search words match what you are looking for. Many of these games and tools are FREE. Here is a snapshot few results that were returned from a search we did in January 2016:

Lab Aids | Science Kits and Materials for Middle School ...
lab-aids.com/ ▾
Publishers of Middle and High School science curriculum, custom science kits ... our LAB-AIDS kits and modules have been helping science teachers to prepare
Middle School - High School - Kits & Modules - Your State

Free 9-12 Teacher Resources | Teachers | Digital textbooks ...
https://www.discoveryeducation.com/teachers/free-9-12-teacher-resources/ ▾
Free high school teacher resources for grades 9-12, including puzzlemaker ... such as sustainability, farming, economics, and the new science behind farming

Ten Websites for Science Teachers | Edutopia
www.edutopia.org/.../websites-for-science-teachers-eric-brunsell ▾ Edutopia ▾
Feb 7, 2012 - From teaching resources for the nature of science and authentic field ... Check out Planting Science to connect your middle or high school

Your High School Classroom - National Science Teachers ...
www.nsta.org/highschool/ ▾ National Science Teachers Association ▾
Attention high school science teachers! We need you! ... The staff of NSTA Reports has collected hundreds of free resources for you. Take a moment to browse

---

Self-Attitude Check

Have you ever acted like Jaleesa in school with any situation? Please explain.

_____

_____

Would you say that there is room for improvement in the type of student that you are? What are some specific ways that you can improve?

_____

_____

_____

No one is perfect. We all have something that we can improve about ourselves. Have you ever heard the phrase that you shouldn't put all of your eggs in one basket? It means that if there is something that you really want to happen, you should not just depend solely on one source to help get you what you want. If a good and well-rounded education is what you want, then you should be taking advantage of as many opportunities as possible to learn and grow as a professional student.

There are several FREE out-of-school time programs available to support your learning!

Thousands of agencies in the United States have received money from the government and other financial sources to create FREE educational programs for students. Many of these programs have a hard time finding students to participate in their programs.

The big question is how do you find out about these programs. Each city and school has different ways to communicate what programs are available to their students. A teacher or other school staff person is your best resource for finding out about where and when out-of-school time programs are offered.

The letter on the next page can help you spread the word about your desire to participate in FREE educational programs. It would be good to make a copy, fill in the blanks and give a copy to your teachers, counselors and any other adults that you think might have information on educational programs outside of your regular classes.

LETTER FROM AN EAGER TO LEARN AND GROW STUDENT

Dear _____,

My name is _____. I attend _____ School

and I am in the _____grade. I would like to ask for your help to find supplemental educational

and leadership programs that will help me learn and grow more as a professional student. This

would mean so much to me because I really and truly value learning.

Please let me know when programs become available anytime during the school year.

Thank you so much for all you do for me and for students like me. Your kindness goes a long

way in helping to ensure that my future is bright.

Sincerely yours,

Student name _____ Date: _____

My phone number: _____ Email: _____

Overcrowded classrooms

It can be difficult for students to concentrate on learning in an overcrowded classroom. Likewise, it is also very challenging for a teacher to hold the attention of everyone in the class, especially when it is overcrowded. Let's take a peek inside Ms. Smith 6th hour English class. Ms. Smith has a total of forty-six 10th grade students.

Front of the Class

The class tardy bell rings.

"Good morning Ms. Smith. I did my homework and I have a few questions on the assignment," said Robert enthusiastically as he prepares to take his seat right next to Ms. Smith's desk.

"That is wonderful Robert and hopefully we can get to your questions today." Ms. Smith replied as she stood quickly to usher the rest of the students in to take their seats.

The room gradually became louder and louder as more students entered the room. There are loud conversations, laughter and books banging on the desks.

"Class please come in quietly and take your seats," said Ms. Smith repeatedly in a voice loud enough to be heard over all of the noise.

About 20 minutes into the class hour, Ms. Smith finally is able to get everyone in their seats. Many students, however, are still holding their own side conversations, but just not as loudly as before.

Robert and 3 other students always sit right next to Ms. Smith's desk. They have found that this is the best way to get the attention they need to learn in a classroom with so many students.

With only about 30 minutes of class time left, Ms. Smith walks over to Robert's desk. "Alright Robert, thank you for being so patient as usual. Please show me what you needed more help with," she said.

The other 3 students sitting next to Robert listen attentively to Ms. Smith as she answers Robert's questions since they all had the same questions as he did.

Meanwhile, the rest of the class continues to talk in their own separate conversations about things that have nothing to do with school or English class.

Food for thought:

When you are in class, it can be very difficult to avoid getting caught up in the side conversation going on in the classroom, especially if you are naturally a very talkative person. Too much talking during class time about unrelated things can make you miss out on learning basic academic lessons that you will need in college.

Why do you believe that Ms. Smith did not spend more time trying to get the entire class's attention so that they could all participate in the learning?

_____

_____

What would you have done if you were Ms. Smith to hold the attention of forty-six 10th grade students in one classroom for an entire hour?

_____

_____

_____

Think about what some of your friends (or you) talk about during class while the teacher is trying to teach. Now explain how the topic of these conversations will help you prepare for subjects taught in college?

_____

_____

How do you think your experience will be in a college English class if you never take advantage of learning the basic English lessons in middle of high school?

_____

_____

Quick Tip

If you truly want to get the best learning experience possible in an overcrowded classroom, the best way to do it is to sit as close to the teacher as possible. Talk to your teacher and ask questions when you don't understand something. This is the best way to let them know that you have an interest in learning. The further away you sit, the more tempting it is to lose focus and join in meaningless side conversation. You have plenty of time to socialize during lunch, in the hall or after school, but you have less than an hour to get the education that will actually benefit you once you leave high school.

There may be times when you have close friends in your class which make it harder for you to concentrate. Have you ever heard the quote, "Show me your friends and I will show you your future?"

What do you think this quote means and in what ways do you think that it might apply to you?

_____
_____
_____

Are you a leader or a follower?

_____

If you chose leader, then your friend should follow your positive behavior. And if you chose that you are a follower, then you should be following a friend that shows positive behaviors. It is important to be honest here because if you are a follower and have friends with negative behaviors, then it is definitely time to find some new friends.

Why is it important to have positive friends, especially if you are a follower?

_____
_____

You should not feel bad, if you are a follower. No one is born a leader. Leadership is something that people grow into as they develop educationally, emotionally and professionally.

So, what might the possible outcomes be for you based on the decisions that you are making right now. Let's take a look at the outcomes in the near future of Jaleesa and Robert if they continue making the same decisions.

Robert and Jaleesa Go to College

Great news! Robert and Jaleesa both eventually graduate and go on to college.

Robert learned all he could in high school and graduated with a 3.8 G.P.A. He attended a local community college. College was very fun for Robert. The classes were not easy, but at least he was able to understand what was being taught. Robert felt like he fit in perfectly with the educational level of his classmates in college.

Jaleesa also graduated from high school. Her high school G.P.A. was a 1.8. She bullied other students into helping her cheat her way through high school.

Jaleesa had missed at least 8 days of school every month since 9th grade. As a result, she missed a lot of educational time in high school.

Jaleesa's classmates in college quickly picked up on her low reading and math level by the incorrect answers that she frequently gave whenever the teacher called on her in class. As a result, whenever there was a group project, no one wanted Jaleesa in their group. Students were friendly towards her, but when it came to serious classwork, they frequently avoided working or studying with her. It costs money to go to college, therefore many students took learning in college very seriously.

After the first few weeks of class, Jaleesa started to feel embarrassed and secluded by the students in her class. College was boring to her because she did not understand the material and no one wanted to work with her on class assignments. She was too embarrassed to ask for tutoring because she didn't like the feeling of appearing dumb to the college tutors.

Jaleesa decided that college was not for her and stopped going.

Robert completed college 7 years later and became a Family Lawyer at the age of 25.

Food for thought:

Why do you believe that Robert was successful in college?

_____

_____

Why do you believe Jaleesa was not as successful in college as Robert?

_____

_____

Why do you believe no one wanted Jaleesa in their group?

_____

What do you believe Jaleesa did next after dropping out of college? What would you have done next?

_____

_____

_____

What could Jaleesa have done differently in high school that might have made college life easier for her?

_____

_____

Your Take Away

Considering all of the discussions from Step 1, is there any situation in your own life that you can use to relate to the discussions in this step? Please explain.

_____

_____

_____

_____

_____

_____

_____

_____

_____

_____

Step 2: Don't let your environment determine your future

"The world will not be destroyed by those who do evil, but those who watch them without doing anything." —
Albert Einstein

Think about your environment, more specifically about your family and your neighborhood. Is it relatively safe where you live or is there a lot of crime in your neighborhood? Do many people in your family have a college education or will you be among the first in your family to go to college and finish? Would you say that your family is doing okay financially? No need to answer this aloud, but just some things to think about as we begin discussions related to this step.

It may seem like there are constant forces from the outside working against your success. Maybe you feel like your parents are against you. The truth is that people usually have a reason behind everything they do. If it is your peers, they could be jealous of you, especially if they secretly feel like you are better than them because you are very pretty or smart. If it is your parents that you feel are against you, then it may be because they are frustrated with something that you are doing or not doing which could affect your future in a bad way. They may also just be overwhelmed with all the responsibilities of needing to provide for a family. We are all human and have our own individual issues or problems, so it is important to remember this when thinking about all of the people in your life.

Family emotional challenges

Robert and Jaleesa are an excellent example of how two people can come from the same family background, but have very different outcomes in life based simply on the choices they have made early on.

23

Robert and Jaleesa are brother and sister. They both were born and raised in the exact same single parent home and neighborhood in the Detroit, Michigan. The choices that they each made in high school eventually lead them in two different directions. Robert became a lawyer and at this point, we are not sure what happened to Jaleesa after dropping out of college.

It is important that we get a better understanding of the one person that they have both had in their lives since the day they were born, their Mom, Latonia Williams.

Shattered Heart

Hi, my name is Latonia Williams. On October 23, 1999, I was so happy to finally be engaged to the man of my dreams, my children's father, Robert McDaniel Senior. We dated for 5 years and we had one son, Robert Jr. and little baby girl on the way. I still remember as if it was yesterday. I was nine months pregnant with our second child who we had decided to name Jaleesa.

Robert Sr. was always a good boyfriend and father. He gave me money whenever I needed it and always made sure Robert Jr. was dressed to impress. I am still not exactly sure how Robert Sr. made his money because he didn't have a job. Despite the fact that he had money, Robert Sr. decided that he preferred a small wedding, so we were going to just do a fast drive to the courthouse to get married. While I was running around the apartment trying to find my shoes so that we could leave to go get married, my water broke! Robert Sr. took me to the hospital immediately. I gave birth to a beautiful 8 lb. baby girl and named her Jaleesa Olivia.

The next morning at the hospital, I was so excited to wake up and hold my baby girl Jaleesa. I wiped the sleep from my eyes and looked around the room, but did not see the baby. Robert Sr. had taken Jaleesa to the hospital nursery before he left last night so that I could get some rest. He is so thoughtful.

I looked to the far left of me and saw a beautiful young woman sitting in the chair next to my hospital bed just staring at me. She looked like she might have been about nine months pregnant too.

The room was silent. Her stare would not leave me, then suddenly she rubbed her stomach and her eyes filled with water. Two tears simultaneously rolled down her cheeks.

Just then Robert Sr. walked in the room and looked in total surprise and shock at both of us. He assumed that Donya (the woman sitting in the chair) had already told me. He walked over to Donya, took her hand to help her out of the chair, wiped the tears from her eyes and they began to walk out of the room hand in hand. Robert Sr. looked back at me and said, "I'm sorry, but I need a fresh start. I really haven't been happy with you for a long time." I laid there in complete shock with my mouth wide open. That was the day he left me for Donya. I later found out that he had been seeing her for more than 2 years while we were together.

I sat in my hospital bed in complete disbelief of what had just happened. Just then, the nurse brought Jaleesa back into the room. Suddenly, all of the joy of having a new baby had unconsciously walked right out of the door with Robert Sr. and the woman that became his wife later that same day.

It is so hard to force myself to be happy and everyday feels like a struggle. Ever since that day I have smoked marijuana or drank alcohol to continually escape the pain that I wake up and feel each day that I look at my daughter. She has unintentionally become a constant reminder of that day. I want to set a better example for my kids, but I am just so full of anger and resentment.

Food for thought:

How do you believe Robert Sr. made his money? Why do you think that?

_____

_____

Latonia said that Robert was a good father and boyfriend. Her reason for saying this was because he gave her money whenever she wanted it and bought Robert Jr. nice clothes. Is this all it takes to be a good father and boyfriend? Why or why not?

_____

_____

_____

What kind of example is Mom setting for her kids by smoking and drinking to escape problems of life? Why?

_____

_____

_____

Why do you believe that Mom is always filled with anger and resentment? Does smoking marijuana or drinking help to make things better? Why or why not?

_____

_____

_____

Did Robert Sr. handle the situation like a man when he walked in and saw the two women? Why or why not? How should he have handled it?

_____

_____

_____

Mom is only able to see the negative depressing part of her children's father leaving her for another woman. What might the positive side of him leaving be?

_____

_____

_____

_____

Do you believe that what happened might affect Mom's relationship with her children as they grow older? If yes, in what ways do you believe it will affect the relationship and why?

_____

_____

_____

_____

What type of things would you suggest Mom do to help herself heal so that she can get over this traumatic heartbreak?

_____

_____

_____

Quick Tip

If you ever find yourself or loved ones experiencing a pain so deep that it interferes with normal day to day life, you can always seek out counseling through a church, school or health provider. Counseling or joining a support group can help people whose lives have been turned upside down by emotional trauma and depression.

Using drugs and alcohol to drown out problems

The stressors that come with not being able to afford food, clothing or housing for your family can be overwhelming for anyone. In cities like Detroit drugs and alcohol are very easy to get to and can often be found within a mile of a person's home. Increased drug (i.e. marijuana) and alcohol use often leads to broken and dysfunctional families.

Some parents encourage their teens to drink and smoke with them. Do you believe this is wise? Why or why not?

_____

_____

_____

Drugs and alcohol will never make problems go away in the real world. Instead, these substances help you to ignore and forget about any problems you have, which allows these same problems to continue to pile up and get worse. When your "high" goes down, your problems are still there.

Are there many marijuana or liquor stores near where you live? Do you think that this is good for your community? Why or why not?

_____

_____

Drinking alcohol and smoking marijuana alters your ability to think clearly.

There is a myth that most teens use marijuana; this is completely false. Most teens do not use marijuana. So, if you are told that everyone is using it, don't believe it.

Below are a few facts about the use of marijuana.

Fact #1: Marijuana and alcohol use can be addictive.

Fact #2: After alcohol, marijuana is the drug most often linked to car accidents, including those involving deaths.

Fact #3: Research shows that marijuana is linked to school failure. Students who use marijuana are more likely to get low grades and dropout of high school.

Fact #4: Research shows that you can lower your Intelligence Quotient (IQ) by smoking marijuana.

Fact #5: High doses of marijuana can cause psychosis or panic when you are high. Psychosis is having disturbed perception and thoughts.

Fact #6: Regular use of marijuana has been linked to depression, anxiety and loss of drive and motivation.

Fact #7: Drinking alcohol can raise your risk of getting cancer.

What other types of things have you heard about smoking marijuana or drinking alcohol?

_____

_____

What value do you see smoking or drinking alcohol adding to your own life now and beyond high school?

_____

_____

_____

Challenges of parenting a teen

As Jaleesa and Robert got older, raising them seemed to be more and more of a challenge for Latonia to do alone. Her children are a constant reminder of how badly their father had hurt her many years ago. Jaleesa especially, brings up her father and his wife, Donya's name a lot. Latonia hates this, but Jaleesa is a Daddy's girl. Robert Sr. spoils her rotten and gives her whatever she wants.

One day Jaleesa's Mom was trying to wake her up to get ready for school. Let's see what happened next.

Shattered Phone

"Time to get up for school, Jaleesa, said Mom. "You're going to be late."

"I'm not going. That stupid teacher, Ms. Smith suspended me again today because of my cell phone," Jaleesa replied.

"You are nothing but trouble! I have to go to work and I can't sit home and babysit or worry about what you are doing every day. Why can't you be more like Robert. I can't wait for you to get out of my house. Give me your phone!"

"Daddy and Donya gave me this phone. They will get mad if you take it and start using it like you did before."

Jaleesa's Mom could not afford a cell phone of her own, so by frequently taking Jaleesa's phone, she was able to have a phone to use.

Suddenly, Jaleesa's Mom could feel the blood rushing through her veins and her heart breaking all over again.

Before she knew it, her Mom had snatched the phone from Jaleesa and threw it against the wall, shattering it into little pieces.

Food for thought:

What do you think about what Jaleesa's Mom said to her when she found out that she was suspended from school?

_____

_____

How do you think this made Jaleesa feel?

_____

_____

Do you believe that she is a bad mother? Why or why not?

_____

_____

Do you believe that her Mom was right for breaking her phone? Why or why not?

_____

_____

How would you have handled the situation if you were Jaleesa's Mom?

_____

_____

_____

Family financial challenges

Without receiving an adequate education beyond high school it can be very difficult to obtain a job, which can earn enough money to financially provide for an entire family and pay the bills. Robert and Jaleesa's Mom dropped out of high school when she got pregnant with Robert. At the time, Latonia believed that their father would take care of them all for the rest of their lives.

Robert Jr. has always felt like he should share some of the blame for his Mom not graduating from high school. He felt like it was his responsibility to make sure that his Mom and sister were taken care of. But just how he made sure that happened was a mystery to everyone except Robert.

Do you think that Robert should feel responsible for his Mom not getting a full education? Why or why not?

_____

_____

_____

Robert the Money Man

"Hey Mom, I'm home. What's for dinner?" shouted Robert as he walked in the door from school.

"I'm sorry baby, but I didn't get time to get by the store today. You and Jaleesa will have to eat bologna sandwiches, crackers and water again," replied Mom.

Robert knew that the truth was she did not have the money to buy more food and she was too proud to ask their father. Robert's Mom was able to get bologna, bread and crackers from the food pantry a couple blocks away from where they live for free.

Robert pulled out a thick roll of $10 bills and counted out $50 to give to his Mom to go get some food.

"Robert, you know that you don't have to keep giving money to me like this. You work hard for this and I know they don't pay you much at that fast food place. Plus, you only make $8.15 an hour working, 10 hours a week. I feel bad taking your little money for food and sometimes bills all the time," said Mom.

Robert leaned down to kiss his short Mom on the forehead. "No worries, Mom, your baby boy got your back. I'm going to always take care of my Mama."

Robert walked away and into the room where he could hear Jaleesa was crying over her shattered phone, which was now in pieces all over the floor. He reached down in another pocket and pulled out a thick roll of $20 bills. Robert counted out $80 to give to Jaleesa.

"Here you are Sis. Stop the crying and go get yourself another phone, but just don't tell Mom." Robert stood there holding up the money until Jaleesa promised not to tell.

"I promise!" Jaleesa said, now smiling ear to ear.

Food for thought:

It is obvious that Robert is doing more than simply working at a fast food place, especially if he only works 10 hours per week. What else do you think he might be doing?

_____

_____

_____

_____

Why do you think that his Mom does not question him more about why he has so much money?

_____

_____

_____

Do you believe that Mom only uses Robert's money for food and bills or are there other things that she might be using it for? Explain.

_____

_____

What are some honest and legal ways that Robert could earn money?

_____

_____

_____

Often young people with very little experience in the way real life works will want to choose the easiest way possible to make money, regardless of whether it is legal or not. Making money illegally will nearly always lead you behind bars or worse.

Robert has found an easy way to make money, but it is not by selling drugs or doing anything illegal. Robert is a business person. He has a Spiderman character business. Parents of small children hire him to dress up as Spiderman for birthday parties and kids' events. He charges $50 an hour. The kids absolutely love him and Robert has a lot of fun playing with them.

In Robert's English class the teacher gave the class a business template assignment to start their own business. Although he completed his class assignment based on a Spiderman Character Business; he has never told anyone that he went on and actually started doing the business. Robert is afraid that he will be looked at as weird, gay or childish for dressing up like a superhero, so he prefers to not tell his friends or his Mom.

The next page shows Robert's completed business template. Let's see how much money Robert is able to make on average from his Spiderman Character business.

Do you think that Robert is weird or childish for dressing up like a Superhero? Why or why not?

_____

_____

Some examples of other businesses that you could start include babysitting, doing hair, mowing lawns, shoveling snow, baking cookies, etc. You can use the business template on the next couple of pages to brainstorm your own business ideas. You may want to make blank copies first, so that you can use this template as many times as you need to.

Business start-up template sample

1. Business name:	Spiderman Character Business	2. *Target market (Who do you think will want to buy your product or service? These are the people that you want to advertise your business to.)	Parents of children ages 4-9

3. How are you going to advertise your business? Word of mouth, Facebook, Youtube videos of parties with me acting like Spiderman. Passing out my flyers on Sunday to Moms of small kids at the churches in my neighborhood.

4. What start-up costs do you have? Costume (bought for $50 at a resale shop), music CD with Spiderman theme song and dance party music for small kids (bought for $5 at a garage sale).

	Service/Product	*Service/Product*	*Service/Product*
5. What type of services/products will you offer? List them here:	Game 1: Help Spiderman search for the hidden treasures (2 hours)	Game 2: Spiderman hide-n-seek (2 hours)	Spiderman dance party (2 hours)
6. Cost of goods sold (How much do the supplies cost to help you perform the service or make this product?)	$20 for 20 treasure items from the dollar store	No need to buy anything to play this game	No need to buy anything to play this game
7. For each service/product, will you charge by the hour or just a flat rate?	○Flat Rate (stays the same) ●Per hour (changes based on the number of hours)	○Flat Rate (stays the same) ●Per hour (changes based on the number of hours)	○Flat Rate (stays the same) ●Per hour (changes based on the number of hours)
8. If you chose flat rate, list how much you will charge for each service/product. If you chose per hour, list how much you will charge per hour.	Flat Rate $_____ Per hour $50	Flat Rate $_____ Per hour $50	Flat Rate $_____ Per hour $60
9. How many hours/days do you plan to work?	2 hours on Saturday	2 hours on Saturday	2 hours on Sunday
10. Gross Income (Multiply the flat/per hour rate in #8 by your answers to #9)	$ 100.00	$ 100.00	$ 120.00
11. How much total will you Gross each week (Add all amounts in row #10)?	$ 320.00		
12. Net Profit (Subtract #6 from #10)	$ 80.00	$ 100.00	$ 120.00
13. How much will your Net Profit be each week? (This is how much you keep for yourself. Add all amounts in row #12)	$ 300.00		

Business start-up template blank

1. Business name:		2. *Target market (Who do you think will want to buy your product or service? These are the people that you want to advertise your business to.)	
3. How are you going to advertise your business?			
4. What start-up costs do you have?			
	Service/Product	*Service/Product*	*Service/Product*
5. What type of services/products will you offer? List them here:			
6. Cost of goods sold (How much do the supplies cost to help you perform the service or make this product?)			
7. For each service/product, will you charge by the hour or just a flat rate per job?	○Flat Rate (stays the same) ○Per hour (changes based on the number of hours)	○Flat Rate (stays the same) ○Per hour (changes based on the number of hours)	○Flat Rate (stays the same) ○Per hour (changes based on the number of hours)
8. If you chose flat rate, list how much you will charge for each service/product. If you chose per hour, list how much you will charge per hour.	Flat Rate $_____ Per hour $_____	Flat Rate $_____ Per hour $_____	Flat Rate $_____ Per hour $_____
9. How many hours/days do you plan to work?			
10. Gross Income (Multiply the flat/per hour rate in #8 by your answers to #9)	$ _____	$ _____	$ _____
11. How much total will you Gross each week (Add all amounts in row #10)?	$ _____		
12. Net Profit (Subtract #6 from #10)	$ _____	$ _____	$ _____
13. How much will your Net Profit be each week? (This is how much you keep for yourself. Add all amounts in row #12)	$ _____		

Quick Tip

Once you become an adult, you will need to make your business legal by paying business taxes and abide by the guidelines and rules that your state has made for businesses like yours. If you are interested in taking your business to the next level after graduating high school, you can visit the small business administration website to find resources in your local area that can help you legally set up your own business www.sba.gov

Neighborhood crime and safety

Another thing that usually comes to mind when we think of environment is the way our neighborhood looks. Have you ever been to another area outside of where you live where it may have looked much different? Perhaps it was cleaner or there were not as many liquor or marijuana stores. Maybe there were other differences that you noticed.

If you answered yes, what were some of the major differences that you noticed between your neighborhood and the one that you visited?

_____

_____

_____

Robert and Jaleesa live in one of the most dangerous areas of Detroit where more than half of the houses are boarded up or burned down. Crime was so high in their zip code of 48205 that it was considered the most dangerous city in America a few years ago.

The city government is responsible for making sure that burned down or abandoned homes are not left open and dangerous. However, many cities, like Detroit, do not have the resources available to manage the numerous open and dangerous properties because many of the same properties are repeatedly vandalized or burned every day.

Have you ever witnessed someone damaging an abandoned boarded up house? What did you do? Why?

_____

_____

Buildings that are left opened and abandoned become dangerous places when people use them for illegal activities. Let's see what happens when Jaleesa is taken to an abandoned house.

Jaleesa & The Abandoned House

As Jaleesa was walking through her neighborhood on her way to school, she met this really cute, well dressed guy. He was 22-year-old, smooth talking Anthony Waller.

"Hey there beautiful. Where are you heading to? Can I give you a ride?" asked Anthony as he drove along side of Jaleesa in his brand new black Dodge Durango with sparkling silver spree-wells on every tire.

Jaleesa politely declined his offer.

"No thank you," she said blushing with a smile.

Anthony stopped, parked and locked up his car, then got out to walk alongside Jaleesa.

"Well, I just can't keep driving while such a gorgeous woman walks, so I will walk with you. My name is Anthony and what is your name, Sweetness."

"My name is Jaleesa, but I am already running a little late for school. This is my first day back after being suspended for 3 days."

Suddenly, a car with dark tented windows stopped in the middle of the street and rolled down one window. Anthony and Jaleesa watched the car approaching. They both caught a glimpse of an object pointing out of the window that looked like a gun! Anthony grabbed Jaleesa's hand and took off with her running between 2 vacant houses and down the alley. They ended up at an abandoned house.

Once inside, Jaleesa noticed that there was a tattered couch and bed in the living room area, which both looked like they were recently used. She also noticed a cooler on the floor beside the couch. Anthony invited Jaleesa to sit on the bed and handed her a bottle of water from the cooler on the floor as she was gasping for air and tried to catch her breath.

"Wow, that was a close one. Are you alright, Beautiful?" Anthony asked as he rubbed Jaleesa's back.

"No, I am still a little shaken up, that was very scary."

"Do you smoke?" Anthony asked as he searched for a match to light his marijuana cigar.

He quickly continued talking, purposely not allowing her time to answer, "Whenever, I am nervous or have a lot on my mind, smoking always helps to calm me down and make me feel more relaxed."

Jaleesa looked at the clock.

"I really need to get to school. Maybe I can give you my number and you can call me later," Jaleesa said as she looked around and began to feel uncomfortable.

"You said that you haven't been there in over 3 days, one more day is not going to hurt you. Everybody deserves some relaxation time. Here, take a puff of this and relax. You are the most beautiful and intelligent woman I have ever met. I'm really shaken up a lot too and could really use the company of someone like you," Anthony said as he held the cigar that he had been smoking up to Jaleesa's mouth.

Jaleesa took one small puff and blew out the smoke.

Food for thought:

What do you believe happens next? Do you believe that Jaleesa ever made it to school that day?

_____
_____
_____

Do you believe that the whole situation with the mysterious dark tented windows car could have been a setup to give Anthony an opportunity to lure Jaleesa back to the seemingly abandoned house? Why or why not?

_____
_____
_____

What do you believe that Anthony's true intentions were with Jaleesa? What makes you believe that these are his true intentions?

_____
_____
_____

Do you believe that it was a wise decision for Jaleesa to smoke marijuana with Anthony? Why or why not?

_____

_____

Jaleesa likely did not realize how old Anthony was. She is in the 9th grade and 15 years old. In your opinion, is there anything wrong or illegal about her dating a 22-year-old man? If yes, what is wrong or illegal about it?

_____

_____

_____

What would you suggest that Jaleesa had done differently to prevent being in the situation that she is in now with Anthony?

_____

_____

_____

Most dangerous cities in America

With this section you may need to review together as a group, then take time to do some research. Return to the Restorative Circle after everyone has done some research to answer and discuss the questions in more detail.

In many cities across America shootings and the sound of gunshots are very common. According to Federal Bureau of Investigations (FBI) Uniform Crime Report, Jaleesa and Robert's hometown of Detroit, Michigan, topped the list again in 2014 as having the highest crime rate in the nation with a population of over 200,000.

Do you feel safe where you live? Why of why not? What makes you feel safe?

_____

_____

On the following pages you will see detailed crime statistics for each of the cities that made the Top 10 List Most Dangerous Cities [with a population] Over 200,000 in 2014. The data was gathered between January 2014 – December 2014.

As you look at the crime statistics for Detroit below, pay special attention to the Officer to Population Ratio. This number tells you how many police officers there are for every specific set of people. For example, in Detroit, the Officer to Population Ratio is 1:295. This means that for every 295 people that live in Detroit, there is only 1 police officer available help them.

#1 Detroit, Michigan
Violent crime rate: 1,989/100,000 people
Murder rate: 44/100,000 people
Population: 684,694 people
Officer to population ratio: 1:295
Rank last year: #1

Would this Officer to Population Ratio make you feel safe if you lived in Detroit? Why or why not?

_____

_____

You may be very surprised to know, just like we were, that the data below landed Irvine, California as the #1 Safest City in America with a population over 200,000.

#1 Safest City - Irvine, California
Violent crime rate: 49/100,000
Murder rate: 0/100,000
Population: 242,971
Officer to Population Ratio: 1:1,215
Rank last year: #1

Remember the Officer to Population Ratio was 1 officer for every 295 people in Detroit. How do you think Irvine is able to continue to hold the top spot as the safest city in America with **only 1 police officer for every 1,215 people**?

_____

_____

_____

Do some research on Irvine, California to find more about why Irvine is able to be considered the safest city in the Nation. You can begin your research by finding answers to the following questions for discussion.

What is the average family household income per year? _____ (Link to the U.S. Census Bureau QuickFacts can be accessed at www.youthworkbook.com)

The median annual family income is around $26,000 in Detroit. You can find your city's annual family income from the U.S. Census Bureau as well.

How might household income be related to the amount of crime in a neighborhood?

_____

_____

_____

Do you believe that education plays any role in how safe the city is? Please explain.

_____

_____

_____

What if anything, can you do in the future to help improve the safety of your own community? The future can be in the very near future or after you graduate from high school or college.

_____

_____

_____

_____

Top Ten Most Dangerous Cities with a Population Over 200,000

#1 Detroit, Michigan
Violent crime rate: 1,989/100,000 people
Murder rate: 44/100,000 people
Population: 684,694 people
Officer to population ratio: 1:295
Rank last year: #1

#2 Memphis, Tenessee
Violent crime rate: 1,741/100,000 people
Murder rate: 21/100,000 people
Population: 654,922 people
Officer to population ratio: 1:293
Rank last year: #3

#3 Oakland California
Violent crime rate: 1,685/100,000 people
Murder rate: 20/100,000 people
Population: 409,994 people
Officer to population ratio: 1:573
Rank last year: #2

#4 St. Louis, Missouri
Violent crime rate: 1,679/100,000 people
Murder rate: 50/100,000 people

Population: 318,574 people
Officer to population ratio: 1:230
Rank last year: #4

#5 Birmingham, Alabama
Violent crime rate: 1,588/100,000 people
Murder rate: 25/100,000 people
Population: 212,115 people
Officer to population ratio: 1:245
Rank last year: #8

#6 Milwaukee, Wisconsin
Violent crime rate: 1,476/100,000 people
Murder rate: 15/100,000 people
Population: 600,374 people
Officer to population ratio: 1:318
Rank last year: #7

#7 Baltimore, Maryland
Violent crime rate: 1,339/100,000 people
Murder rate: 34/100,000 people
Population: 623,513 people
Officer to population ratio: 1:224
Rank last year: #6

#8 Cleveland, Ohio
Violent crime rate: 1,334/100,000 people
Murder rate: 16/100,000 people
Population: 388,655 people
Officer to population ratio: Not Available
Rank last year: #5

#9 Stockton, California
Violent crime rate: 1,331/100,000 people
Murder rate: 49/100,000 people
Population: 299,519 people
Officer to population ratio: 1:807
Rank last year: #25

#10 Indianapolis, Indiana
Violent crime rate: 1,255/100,000 people
Murder rate: 16/100,000 people
Population: 858,238 people
Officer to population ratio: 1:559
Rank last year: Unavailable

If you are not able to locate your cities crime statistics on the previous pages or if you would like to find data for another year, you can find your city's crime data by following the links located at www.YouthWorkbook.com or by following these instructions:

1. Go to www.FBI.gov
2. Hold your cursor over "About Us"
3. Click on "Criminal Justice Information Services" in the drop down menu that appears
4. On the page, Click on "Crime Statistics/UCR" to the right
5. Under Publications, click on "Crime Statistics in the United States"
6. Now you should be on the Uniform Crime Reports page. Under Crime in the United States, click on the year of interest to you.
7. Now you should be on the About Crime in the U.S. page. To find violent crime rate click on "Violent Crime," under Offenses Known to Law Enforcement.
8. Click to Browse by "State Totals"
9. To find Officer to Population Ratio information return to the About Crime in the U.S. page. Next click on "Go to Police Employee Tables" located under Police Employee Data.
10. Under Data Tables, click on data "Table 78"
11. Click on your state of interest and scroll down the list until you come to your city of interest.

Ranking information needs to be calculated using various reports from this website. It can be very complicated and requires professional help to compare and analyze the data in order to determine ranking.

You may be wondering what can you do right now to help lower crime in your own neighborhood. As a youth, here are a list of things that you can do now. Discuss how doing each one of these things could help to lower crime in your own neighborhood.

1. Know what the number is to make an anonymous crime report if you see a crime occurring or about to occur and be sure to use it. Keep this number with you at all times. What is the number? _____
2. Encourage your parents to exchange phone numbers with as many neighbors as possible so that they can alert one another of possible criminal activity taking place on their property or in the neighborhood.
3. Never walk with your head down in your phone. Always be aware of your surroundings so that you will be aware of possible crime going on around you.
4. Volunteer with nonprofit or public organizations whose mission is to stop crime in your neighborhood.

Here are some tips that you can use to help keep yourself out of legal trouble. Explain how each of the items below can help to keep you out of trouble.

1. Be in your house before your legal curfew time.

   _____

   _____

2. Don't hang out in or around abandoned property.

   _____

   _____

3. Don't consume illegal substances like any type of drugs or alcohol and don't hang out with kids that are doing these things.

   _____

   _____

4. Don't be near kids that are participating in any kind of illegal activity (i.e. theft, vandalism, fighting, etc.

   _____

   _____

By allowing your environment to control your emotions and decision-making, you are doing more harm to your future than good. The older you become, the more you will find that there is a consequence for every decision that you make. If you refuse to let your environment control your ability to make good decisions, you will be on a great path to creating a brighter future for you and your own children.

As you may have assumed Jaleesa never made it to school that day when she met Anthony. Actually, she didn't make it to school for the next 2 days either. She ended up falling into a deep infatuation with Anthony. Jaleesa of course felt that it was love. Jaleesa spent the days that she was supposed to be in school, with Anthony smoking marijuana and performing other risky activities in the abandoned house. Jaleesa attempted to return to school on Monday morning. Let us see what happened.

Kicked Out Again & Again

"Well Good Morning Jaleesa, welcome back. Can I please see your re-admittance slip?" asked Ms. Smith.

Jaleesa gave Ms. Smith a crumbled up slip of paper and an absence excuse note that she had written earlier that morning.

"This re-admittance slip is dated for your return on Wednesday of last week! I will need to speak with your parent to verify your absence excuse for the last 3 days before you can re-enter class. You need to report to the main office," Ms. Smith stated.

"I am not leaving. I just gave you my absence excuse!" Jaleesa exclaimed loudly.

Ms. Smith picked up the phone to call security and have Jaleesa physically removed from the classroom. Jaleesa became irate, stood up and turned over her desk in an angry rage.

"F… you! You ugly B….!" Jaleesa shouted as she walked out of the room.

Security was walking down the hall towards the room as Jaleesa walked out of the class. They observed Jaleesa shouting profanities and verbal threats at Ms. Smith in a rage as she left the room. Security immediately grabbed her arms and placed her in handcuffs before taking her to the main office.

When she arrived to the main office, Jaleesa was still yelling profanities directed at the guards and the school staff. It was very obvious to all who looked on that she was extremely upset. The Principal called Jaleesa's Mom and left a voicemail message that Jaleesa was being put out of school.

Security walked Jaleesa outside of the building, removed her handcuffs and allowed her to go free.

Jaleesa headed straight to the abandoned house where she and her new boyfriend, Anthony, spent most of their time.

Food for thought:

Jaleesa seems to have a much worst temper than she has had in the past. What reasons do you believe could be contributing to her increased temper and her apparent inability to control it?

_____
_____
_____

Do you believe that Jaleesa's behavior is justified? Why or why not?

_____
_____
_____

Robert Gets Robbed

"You did a great job at my son's birthday party, Robert! The kids loved you today as Spiderman," said Ms. Smith. "How much do I owe you?"

"The party actually went a little over 2 hours, but that's ok. I will still just charge you only $50 per hour, so that'll be $100 total," Robert replied.

"Thanks Robert. Here is $125, a little extra for a job well done. You be safe out there. I'll see you Monday at school."

"Thanks, bye," said Robert as he walked out the door of the birthday hall.

Once he reached the corner of the street, Robert stopped to count his money.

"20, 40, 60, 80, 100, 120, 5," he counted aloud to himself.

Anthony, whom Robert had never met, was driving by and noticed Robert counting money. Anthony decided to follow Robert home.

Robert walked around to the side door of his house and put his key in the door. Just then, Anthony jumped out of nowhere and forced himself into the house with Robert at gunpoint! It was late Saturday afternoon and both Jaleesa and their Mother were home.

Robert's Mom screamed to the top of her lungs in fear!

"Get out! Get out! Please don't hurt us! We have nothing to take or give you!" Robert's Mom yelled.

Jaleesa was in the other room and did not know who exactly was in the house or what was happening, but she could feel that something was wrong. Jaleesa called 911 immediately and told them that she thinks someone has just broken into their house.

Robert handed Anthony all of the money in his pocket.

"Here, this is what you want, just take it and leave my family alone," Robert pleaded.

Anthony took the money and put it in his pocket.

"I know you have to have more money and expensive stuff around here somewhere," said Anthony, still pointing the gun at Robert.

Anthony forced Robert at gunpoint to each room of the house while he searched for money and valuables. Next, they entered Jaleesa's room where she was on the phone with 911. Jaleesa looked up in terror.

"Anthony! What are you doing?" Jaleesa exclaimed in disbelief.

"What does it look like I'm doing? Dummy!" Anthony replied as he threw Robert to the ground and made his quick escape through the back door.

Food for thought:

When do you think that Robert should have counted his money to ensure that it was the right amount? Why?

_____

_____

Why do you believe that Anthony followed Robert home instead of robbing him as soon as he saw him counting the money?

_____

_____

Anthony had been so nice to Jaleesa before. Why do you believe he called her a dummy now?

_____

_____

Do you believe that the police ever came? Why or why not?

_____

_____

Your Take Away

Considering all of the discussions from Step 2, is there any situation in your own life that you can use to relate to the discussions in this step? Please explain.

_____

_____

_____

_____

_____

_____

_____

_____

_____

Step 3: Avoid negative peer pressure

"Those who stand for nothing fall for anything." – Alexander Hamilton

When you have low self-esteem, it makes it harder for you to avoid negative peer pressure and negative thoughts about yourself because you just want to fit in and be like everyone else. Peer pressure is not something that you can recognize right away as you will see in the stories that follow.

Dealing with low confidence/self-esteem

There are many reasons that people may suffer from low self-esteem. Sometimes there are situations that we may encounter which makes us have a drop in self-esteem. One example is the effect that the robbery had on Robert. He felt like his manhood had been taken away because he could not protect his family. Having low self-esteem can sometimes make us more susceptible to doing very foolish things.

On Monday at school his teachers noticed that he was not his usual self, often spacing out during class. Ms. Smith sent Robert to the office to see his counselor.

During his visit to the Counseling Office, Robert was asked several questions. Pretend that you are the Counselor. Please explain what your response would be to Robert after you hear each of his responses.

I heard about the home invasion that happened to your family over the weekend. How are you doing Robert?

"I feel like I want to hurt or kill somebody. The guy that robbed us took all the money that we had for food and bills. I am the only man in my house. My Dad is too busy with his other family to really be concerned about my sister, Mom and I. That thief took more than just money, he took my manhood and I want it back! A man is supposed to protect what's his, especially his family. Right? The only way for me to regain my manhood and power is to do some real physical damage to him and I mean really serious damage!" Robert said angrily as he banged his fist on the Counselor's desk.

Counselor (your) response:

_____
_____
_____
_____

Tell me Robert, after you cause this serious physical damage to him, what do you expect to happen next?
I expect that he will learn his lesson and not bother us anymore. But, honestly, I am so angry that I might just really kill him. Then he surely won't bother us anymore.

Counselor (your) response:

_____
_____
_____
_____

If you do kill him, what do you expect will happen next to you?
"I don't know and don't care! All I care about is that he hurt me and my family and he shouldn't have done that!" Robert yelled as he stood and hit the desk even harder with his fist.

The Counselor gave Robert a piercing look of disappointment. Robert has always been one of the school's top academic performing students and a very peaceful student. Robert sat back down slowly, folded his arms on the desk and put his head down in shame.

Robert murmured, "I could go to prison or someone could kill me too."

Counselor (your) response:

_____
_____
_____
_____

What could you do that will help you to get justice without endangering your life or the life of your family?
"I honestly don't know."

Counselor (your) response:

_____
_____
_____
_____

When you have low self-esteem, you compare yourself to others a lot. You never feel like what you have is good enough. People express this feeling in different ways. Some people bully or purposely embarrass others. Many people with low self-esteem take pleasure in seeing others suffer or be down on their luck. Other people with low self-esteem become socially awkward, extremely quiet or socially withdrawn. Socially awkward people with low self-esteem are a perfect target for bullies with low self-esteem. Having the ability to understand this concept is necessary in order to help you get through it.

Do you believe that Jaleesa has high self-esteem? Why or why not?

_____

_____

_____

If Jaleesa had high self-esteem, do you think that she would have fallen so easily for all of Anthony's sweet talk and obvious lies?

_____

_____

_____

Let's take a look at what happened next between Jaleesa and Anthony.

A Dime Piece

On Monday, after physically being put out of school, Jaleesa just walked the streets not knowing where to go. She was still suspended from school and needed her Mom to come see the Principal before she could be readmitted. Her family had just gone through so much over the weekend with the robbery, so she didn't want to upset her Mother with more bad news. She was getting tired of always having to be a disappointment to her mother.

Jaleesa decided to just go to a nearby park to sit and think about how she should handle Anthony.

"How could Anthony do this to me and my family?" she thought to herself as she started to cry intensely. "I love him so much. I wonder if he ever really loved me?"

She pulled out some old tattered papers from her book bag and wiped the snot from her nose.

Suddenly, a light bulb went on in her mind. "Maybe he didn't know that it was my house that he was robbing. He was probably just afraid that I would be angry and break up with him after finding out that he is a thief."

She suddenly felt a small sense of relief and decided to go find Anthony and let him know that she wasn't upset and that she realized that he chose her house by mistake. She ran as fast as she could to their little chill spot at the abandoned house.

When Jaleesa arrived and pushed open the door, she was horrified by what she saw. Anthony was sitting on the couch hugging and kissing Lauren Wright, the most beautiful and popular girl at her school. According to Jaleesa, Lauren had all the qualities that she didn't have and now she also had her boyfriend. Jaleesa felt her heart drop immediately. She just stood there and stared at them both, unable to speak and frozen stiff. At that moment she felt so ugly and useless.

Jaleesa fell to her knees and started crying hysterically, hoping that Anthony would walk over to her, kiss her and apologize for everything.

"Don't you know how to knock? Please get your ugly dusty looking a** out of my house! Can't you see I'm with a dime piece?" Anthony said in a hurtful tone as he laughed at Jaleesa.

Lauren looked at Jaleesa with pity, as though she truly felt sorry for her. Lauren had no idea that Anthony had once messed around with Jaleesa as well.

"I hate you!" Jaleesa yelled. "You will get what you deserve one day."

Anthony jumped up and grabbed Jaleesa by her neck, "Are you threatening me, you little ugly trick?"

"No, no, I'm sorry," Jaleesa murmured as she gasped for air with the snot from her nose now running into her mouth.

Anthony pulled her head closely to his mouth and whispered in her ear, "Remember, I know where you and your entire family live. So you better think long and hard before you threaten me. I could kill you all right now."

Anthony continued to hold her by her neck, opened the door and threw her out of the house, slamming the door behind her.

Lauren looked at Anthony. "Wow, you are such a strong powerful man! That's my baby," she said smiling and blushing from ear to ear.

Food for thought:

Why do you believe that Jaleesa felt a sense of relief when she thought that Anthony had robbed her house by mistake? The fact remains that he was still a thief, but that part didn't seem to upset her as much. Why?

_____
_____
_____

Why did Jaleesa immediately compare her own physical appearance and beauty to Lauren's when she first saw her?

_____

_____

_____

Do you believe that Anthony chose Lauren over Jaleesa strictly because he felt that Lauren was more beautiful? Why or why not?

_____

_____

_____

Did Anthony display the attributes of a strong and powerful man as Lauren suggested? Why or why not?

_____

_____

_____

What do you believe are real attributes of a strong and powerful man?

_____

_____

_____

Why does Jaleesa feel like she is a disappointment to her mother?

_____

_____

_____

The Juvenile Justice System

Needless to say, Jaleesa is extremely distraught over what just happened with Anthony. The very next day, Jaleesa returns to school, but this time she returns with a jealous and hateful vengeance in her heart.

Don't Mess with My Man

"Hey Leesa (Jaleesa), how did you get readmitted back in school? Did your Mom come?" asked Andrea who was Jaleesa's longtime friend since middle school.

Jaleesa looked at her and thought for a moment. She knew what a big mouth Andrea had and how much she liked to gossip, lie and get people in trouble. Jaleesa didn't want to tell her that she had snuck back into school and was actually not supposed to there.

"Yes, she came yesterday so they readmitted me. Guess what?

"What?" asked Andrea moving closer to Jaleesa.

"You know that girl Lauren in our 6th hour class? She has been messing with my man Anthony and think she can take him from me. I can't wait to see her, so I can slap the smile off her face," said Jaleesa.

"Wow, Lauren Wright! Really, all the guys want to get with her. She thinks she is all that. So your boyfriend must have been who I overheard her talking about during lunch today," said Andrea as she looked at Jaleesa out of the corner of her eye, hoping that she would want to know more about what she overheard.

"What did she say about my man?" asked Jaleesa angrily.

"You know I hate gossiping, but you're my girl so I've got to tell you. She was bragging about how she stole this dusty looking girl's boyfriend and how ugly the girl was. She just kept going on and on about it. I had to get to class, so I couldn't stay to listen to more details," said Andrea as she eagerly waited for Jaleesa's angry explosive temper to kick in.

Just then, Andrea caught a glimpse of Lauren walking in the hall where they were standing.

"There that tramp is now!" said Andrea with excitement.

Jaleesa turned around and walked over to Lauren, blocking her path to walk by.

"I heard you been talking about me and my man, you little witch. Why don't you say what you have to say to my face! Or maybe you're scared I'll mess up your tired little weave and makeup?" said Jaleesa.

Lauren laughed.

"Girl please, you are absolutely no threat to me and certainly not worth the time for me to sit around talking about you. I think my man made that pretty clear to you yesterday. Now excuse me," said Lauren rolling her neck and eyes.

What Lauren or no else knew is that Jaleesa had a steel combination lock in her hand. Jaleesa hit Lauren over the head with the lock using all the force and strength she had. Lauren immediately fell to the floor with blood dripping from her head. Jaleesa dropped the lock and ran as fast as she could towards the building exit.

Security heard all of the commotion in the hall and ran over to where Lauren was laying on the floor. The police and ambulance were called immediately.

Security was able to catch Jaleesa before she made it out of the building.

When the police arrived, Jaleesa was arrested and taken to a juvenile detention facility to await sentencing.

Food for thought:

Since Jaleesa knew that Andrea was also a liar, why do you think that Jaleesa immediately believed her?

_____

_____

What kind of self-esteem do you believe Andrea has? Very high, very low or somewhere in between? Why?

_____

_____

Why do you think Jaleesa was still referring to Anthony as her man when speaking to Andrea and Lauren?

_____

_____

Do you think Jaleesa was right or wrong for hitting Lauren? Why? How would you have handled the same situation? Why?

_____

_____

_____

Gun violence

Gun's take lives that can never be brought back. As angry as we all get from time to time, there is no anger that should lead us to take another human life.

Judgement Day

Andrea sent a text message to Robert while he was in class to let him know that the police were handcuffing Jaleesa and about to put her in a squad car. Robert left class immediately and ran outside to find Jaleesa. He spotted her a short distance away being lead to the police car.

"Jaleesa! Jaleesa!," screamed Robert.

"Robert!" Jaleesa yelled back. "Ask Andrea about Anthony, he is the guy that robbed us! He's the reason they are taking me to jail! Everything is all his fault! He is destroying our lives!" Jaleesa continued sobbing in tears.

The police guided her head into the squad car. Before they could shut the door, Jaleesa yelled once more, "Ask Andrea about Anthony!"

When Robert turned around to head back into the school, Andrea was standing right behind him.

"Andrea, who is this dude Anthony and where can I find him?"

Andrea looked puzzled. She thought Jaleesa and Anthony were in love. She didn't know anything about a robbery.

"Oh…um… Anthony…well, all I know is that he always used to take Jaleesa to this abandoned house to hang out and get her high all the time. She missed school for days to go get high with him and do other stuff that I'd rather not say. The house is the blue one on the corner of Avondale and Pembrook," said Andrea with a seemingly concerned look on her face.

"I wish I had a gun right now! I'll show him not to mess with my family," said Robert.

"I know where you can get one easy. You know those guys that are always hanging around the gas station across the street from the school?" said Andrea.

"Yeah," said Robert.

"They can get you more than just drugs and liquor; they can get you a gun too!" said Andrea.

"Bet! said Robert. I'm going over there right now. Please keep this between me and you Andrea, okay?"

"My lips are sealed."

Andrea went to class and immediately after school she went straight to Robert's house to tell his Mom what had happened to Jaleesa and what Robert was planning to do.

Food for thought:

Do you believe Andrea did the right thing by going to tell Robert and Jaleesa's Mom? Why or why not?

_____

_____

If Andrea was truly concerned, why do you believe that she told Robert that Anthony turned Jaleesa on to drugs, where Anthony could be found and exactly how Robert could easily and quickly get a gun?

_____

_____

_____

Why do you believe Jaleesa blamed her own actions and consequences of being arrested on Anthony when she yelled to Robert? Was Anthony truly to blame for her actions?

_____

_____

_____

What gives Robert the authority to end another human being's life? Taking someone's life is something that can never be undone.

_____

_____

How do you feel about guns and how easy it is to obtain one regardless of how old or mentally unstable you are?

_____

_____

_____

What can you do to lessen gun violence in your own community?

_____

_____

_____

Consequences of decisions

Jaleesa's actions at school that day did not go unpunished. Again, with every decision, rather it be good or bad, there is a consequence.

School to Prison

Luckily for Jaleesa, Lauren only sustained minor injuries and was expected to make a full recovery. Jaleesa was only fifteen at the time of the incident where she hit Lauren in the head with a steel lock. In Michigan, juvenile court has original jurisdiction over an individual who is age 16 and younger for law violating behavior. Therefore, juvenile court decided Jaleesa's punishment since she was only 15 at the time. Jaleesa was sentenced to 1-year in a juvenile detention facility for aggravated assault with a weapon and two years of probation where she had to report to a probation officer monthly.

Food for thought:

Do you believe Jaleesa's punishment given by juvenile court was fair? Why or why not?

_____

_____

If not, what punishment would you have given her?

_____

_____

How likely is it for Jaleesa to get into trouble again with law enforcement before she turns 18 if she continues her current bad behaviors and decision-making? Why?

_____

_____

_____

Don't shoot!

Robert had never held or shot a gun before in his life. He was sold a small hand gun on the street for $50.00. The man that sold him the gun showed him the basics of how to aim and fire the gun.

When Robert arrived at the abandoned house, Anthony was standing in the doorway. Anthony recognized him immediately.

"What are you doing around here?" asked Anthony.

Robert continued to walk towards the door, not speaking a word. It was easy to recognize from his facial expression and body language that Robert was very angry.

Robert reached in his pocket for the gun.

Suddenly, two loud gun shots rang out! "Bang, bang!"

About 5 minutes later, Robert's Mom arrived to the house with Andrea, the police and ambulance.

Robert lay on the ground gasping for air, bleeding from his shoulder and left side of his stomach. Anthony had shot him twice, then left the scene.

Food for thought:

Why do you believe that people nowadays choose to fight with guns rather than with their hands? What do you believe is the best way to fight or settle a disagreement? Why?

_____

_____

_____

Why do you think Anthony was able to shoot Robert before Robert was able to shoot him?

_____

_____

How likely do you think it is that the police will put out a citywide search for Anthony and arrest him? Why?

_____

_____

Your Take Away

Considering all of the discussions from Step 3, is there any situation in your own life that you can use to relate to the discussions in this step? Please explain.

_____

_____

_____

_____

_____

_____

_____

Step 4: Discover your purpose in life

"The most dangerous thing in the world is to have no purpose." —Bishop T.D. Jakes

Robert and Jaleesa's Mother was heartbroken, with one child now in a coma in the intensive care unit at the hospital and another in juvenile detention. Latonia blamed herself. She felt as if she had nowhere to turn. It's ironic that prayer is no longer allowed in schools and most public institutions, but it is the first option people turn to when they are in desperate need of help. It is often usually a last resort when alcohol, drugs, social withdrawal/depression are no longer able to drown out the pain. Most people turn to a power that they believe to be greater than themselves and greater than any living being. Just as Latonia did, most people turn to prayer. Latonia sat in her son's hospital room sobbing in tears for days until one day she slid out of her chair to the floor and began to pray.

A Mothers Prayer

Latonia closed her eyes shut. "Dear God, are you there? Can you hear me? I am a failure as a Mother. I didn't mean to be a bad Mother, but this is not something that I wanted to do alone and it just isn't fair. Their father didn't have to deal with them or do anything to help with raising either one of them. Now look what has happened and now everyone is going to look at me like I'm a bad Mother. But none of this is their fault. They didn't ask to be here. Through your blessings, I brought them both here. If you give me and both of them another chance, I promise that I will do better as their Mom. Please show me what you want me to do. Guide me. Please. I will do anything. Anything! Please just help me and my children right now!"

Latonia opened her eyes and Robert was still in a coma and Jaleesa was still in a juvenile center. She felt like she had just wasted her time talking to the walls and that her words did not reach God because she had been such a terrible mother. Suddenly, Latonia felt a calming peace come over her spirit.

She looked up at the wall, saw these words and read them aloud:

"THE PARABLE OF THE SOWER, Matthew Chapter 13:1
THE PARABLE OF THE WHEAT AND THE TARES, Matthew Chapter 13:24
THE PARABLE OF THE MUSTERSEED, Matthew Chapter 13:31"

Food for thought:

Why do you believe that Latonia decided to pray instead of simply going to get high or drunk?

_____
_____
_____

Look up the word "parable" in the dictionary. What does it mean?

_____
_____

The Bible tells the story of a man named Jesus who claimed to be the son of a one true living God speaking in parables. Jesus' parables were all very profound in meaning. Whenever Jesus wanted to give people an important message about life, he told them a parable. Parables have hidden meanings which can be very interesting and enlightening to uncover. Regardless of your religious faith, the parables found in the Bible can be very helpful in helping people get through the trials and tribulations of this thing called life.

The Parable of the Sower

Later that day when Latonia returned home she opened the bible that she had been keeping on top of the fireplace as a decoration. She turned to Matthew Chapter 13, Verse 1 and begin reading aloud. As she read, she thought of the seeds as representing herself and her children.

13 On the same day Jesus went out of the house and sat by the sea.²And great multitudes were gathered together to Him, so that He got into a boat and sat; and the whole multitude stood on the shore.

³Then He spoke many things to them in parables, saying: "Behold, a sower went out to sow. ⁴And as he sowed, some *seed* fell by the wayside; and the birds came and devoured them.

A sower is a person that is putting out seeds to grow them into something meaningful and useful. Instead, the birds came and ate the seeds that the sower had put out before they had a chance to grow. If the seeds represent Latonia and her children, then who or what do you believe would be the bird(s) that devoured them?

_____

Robert and Jaleesa's father could be an example of the bird that devoured the seeds before they could ever get a fair chance to grow. Father's help to rear and raise their children and without that sound foundation in a child's life, children may suffer. This is especially true if the mother is not fully committed to assuming the role of both a mother and a father alone. Their father choosing not to play an active part in raising them not only negatively affected Latonia, but it also affected Robert and Jaleesa in their own ways.

In what ways (if any) do you believe that not having a father help raise them impacted Jaleesa and Robert's decision making?

_____

_____

⁵Some [seeds] fell on stony places, where they did not have much earth; and they immediately sprang up because they had no depth of earth. ⁶But when the sun was up they were scorched, and because they had no root they withered away.

Some people (seeds) fell on hard (stony) places. When the circumstances got to intense (hot like the sun), they were hurt very badly (scorched). Because they had nothing to drive or motivate them to do better (no root), they died and/or their existence became meaningless (withered).

Recall what the hard places were for Robert, Jaleesa and Latonia and how they were each hurt. Explain.

_____

_____

_____

_____

What could each of them have used to drive or motivate them to do better?

_____

_____

_____

_____

⁷And some fell among thorns, and the thorns sprang up and choked them. ⁸But others fell on good ground and yielded a crop: some a hundredfold, some sixty, some thirty. ⁹He who has ears to hear, let him hear!"

Some children were born to dysfunctional families (thorns), which affected (choked) their ability to think and make wise choices as they grew up. Regardless of the kind of family we come from, every person can find "good ground" when we are deeply rooted in a power that is greater than ourselves.

Do you believe that a power exists that is greater than you? Please share more.

_____

_____

What, if anything, can a person that has been born into a dysfunctional family do to prevent themselves from making bad decisions in life?

_____

_____

_____

Now let's see how well you can apply this next parable to the lives of Robert, Jaleesa Latonia and perhaps even yourself.

In the parable that follows, imagine that the following, then answer the questions that follow.

Wheat = A good hearted person

Tares/Weed (a bad weed that looks like wheat but is not) = A bad hearted person who does bad things and purposely hurts others just to get what they want.

The Parable of the Wheat and the Tares

24 Another parable He put forth to them, saying: "The kingdom of heaven is like a man who sowed good seed in his field; 25 but while men slept, his enemy came and sowed tares among the wheat and went his way. 26 But when the grain had sprouted and produced a crop, then the tares also appeared. 27 So the servants of the owner came and said to him, 'Sir, did you not sow good seed in your field? How then does it have tares?' 28 He said to them, 'An enemy has done this.' The servants said to him, 'Do you want us then to go and gather them up?' 29 But he said, 'No, lest while you gather up the tares you also uproot the wheat with them. 30 Let both grow together until the harvest, and at the time of harvest I will say to the reapers, "First gather together the tares and bind them in bundles to burn them, but gather the wheat into my barn."

Food for thought:

The servant asked the sower if he wanted him to go and pull up all of the bad weeds that had grown. The sower did not want him to pull up the weeds because he might accidently pull up the wheat (uproot) in the process.

What would life be like if everyone was good hearted because all the bad hearted people were plucked out of the world and thrown away? Would there be anyone special to you that might be one of the bad hearted people that are plucked away?

_____
_____
_____

If you answered yes to the previous question, then maybe now you can better understand why the bad weeds are not just pulled out from the field in the parable. They are not pulled up because taking them away could negatively impact those that care a lot for them and have good hearts. It is better to wait until the end of their growth then separate the wheat (good people) from the weeds (bad people).

Look up the words "wheat" and "weed" in the dictionary. Metaphorically speaking which would you rather be? Why?

_____

_____

_____

Which do you believe Robert, Jaleesa and Latonia are? A good hearted or bad hearted person? Which would you say you are? Why?

_____

_____

_____

_____

The Parable of the Mustard Seed

[31] Another parable He put forth to them, saying: "The kingdom of heaven is like a mustard seed, which a man took and sowed in his field,[32] which indeed is the least of all the seeds; but when it is grown it is greater than the herbs and becomes a tree, so that the birds of the air come and nest in its branches."

It doesn't matter what kind of family you come from, just like a muster seed you have the potential to grow stronger and wiser. A muster seed is the smallest of all seeds on earth, yet it has the potential to grow so large that birds flock to it and make it their home.

Do you believe that you have finished the mental maturity growing process? Why or why not?

_____

_____

_____

If you answered no, what specific areas do you feel you need to grow more in?

_____

_____

_____

If you grew more in these areas, are there any friends or family members that you believe would support you in your growth? Why or why not?

_____

_____

If you grew more in these areas, who could you be a role model to? Do you have a role model? Do you believe that having a role model is important?

_____

_____

_____

Will you let what others think stop or slow your growth? Why?

_____

_____

Your Take Away

All of these parables have one very important thing in common, they all have roots. A root is very important to growth; without it a seed would not be able to grow. Just like a seed, we need a root as well. You must find your root; your root goes deeper than your history. Your root is the purpose that drives and motivates you to do better.

Latonia's prayers are answered when Robert awakes 30 days later from his coma. Latonia visits him every day and reads the parables to him. She also visits Jaleesa daily and reads the same parables to her. After reading and talking about the parables with them, she asks them both the following questions. Please provide your own answers to these questions.

What is most important, kind of important and least important to you? Write a list.

Most important:

1. _____
2. _____
3. _____

Kind of important:

1. _____
2. _____
3. _____

Least important:

1. _____
2. _____
3. _____

What is your story? For each of the things you named above explain what has happened in your life that makes these things have the level of importance that you placed them in.

_____
_____
_____
_____
_____
_____
_____
_____
_____
_____
_____
_____
_____
_____

Step 5: You must create a plan for yourself

"Unless commitment is made, there are only promises and hopes…but no plans." —Peter Drucker

Robert makes a full recovery and begins to make plans for college. Jaleesa is released from the Juvenile Detention Facility after one year and placed on probation. She continues high school but has fallen even more behind in learning. Recall from Step 1 that Jaleesa decided that college was not for her. Jaleesa decides to enroll in a job training program instead of college. This section of the workbook is what helped them both plan for life after high school.

You may use this section to help you plan for your future too.

Do you know what you want to be when you graduate high school? If not, do not worry because you are not alone. Many students your age have still not made up in their mind what career they would like to do.

Even if you don't know yet, it is still very important that you begin to think about how you will pay for college and how you will support yourself financially while you are in college. Graduating from high school or receiving a General Education Degree (GED) is your first successful step towards continuing your education beyond high school. If you are looking to get full ride scholarships, then your cumulative high school Grade Point Average (GPA) and SAT/ACT scores will be just as important.

Now is the perfect time to think about how you will pay for college or a career-training program. As you think about this, you want to focus on ways that will allow you to avoid going into debt by taking out thousands of dollars in student loans. You may be tempted to take out student loans so that you can get extra money back at the end of each semester and blow it on a lot of materialistic things that you really don't need. This is not a good idea, since you will be expected to pay back every cent of this money. In the long run, it is not worth it. Just be sure to think about this carefully because years down the road, the only person that will be responsible for paying that money back is YOU!

Preparing for college

The planning questions below are helpful for students that plan to attend a community college or university.

You will likely not know the answer to many of these questions right away. We have added the Step 5 Resources link to www.YouthWorkbook.com to help you find answers.

1. What college do you plan to attend?

    _____

    How much is it per credit hour at the college that you would like to attend?

    _____

2. In college, the average class is worth anywhere from 1-4 credits each.

    For each semester, how many credit hours would you like to take total? _____

    Approximately, how many classes is the number of credit hours that you chose equal to? _____

    Will you be considered a full time, ¾ time. ½ time or less than ½ time student?
    _____

    a. full time (approximately 12 credits)
    b. ¾ time (approximately 9-11 credits)
    c. ½ time (approximately 6-8 credits)
    d. Less than ½ time (approximately 1-5 credits)

3. When do you plan to start school? (Month/Year) _____

4. How many college semesters are offered in one year at the college you chose?

    _____

5. You need 62 credits to get an Associate degree. How long will it take you to get an Associate degree based on your answers to #2? _____ (Hint: Multiply the number of credits that you will take each semester by the number of semesters in one

college year. Example: 12 [credits] X 4 [semesters] = 48. So in this example, an Associate degree would take almost 2 years.)

6. An Associate degree is usually the first degree earned in college. What kind of Associate degrees are offered at the college that you would like to attend?

    _____

    _____

    _____

    _____

7. How much will it cost you each college semester to take classes based on the credit hours you selected in #2? *(Hint: Multiply the number of credit hours that you will take in #2 by the cost per credit hour in #1)* _____

8. How much does an average college book cost? _____

    Approximately, how many books will you need based on the number of classes that you will be taking in #2? _____ *(Hint: Count at least 1 book per class)*

    Approximately, how much will you need to spend on books each semester? *(Hint: Multiply the average book cost by how many classes you will take in one semester)*

    _____

9. Are you in a City that gives Promise Scholarships? *(Hint: You can visit www.YouthWorkbook.com and click on the Step 5 Resources link to find out.)*

    If not, you will need to contact the financial aid office at the school of your choice to find out what scholarships may be available to you. Record the phone number/email to the college's financial aid office below.

    _____

    _____

    _____

If you have a low GPA or SAT/ACT Score you may find that you do not qualify for very many scholarships. A great way around this, which many students take is to do their very best in all of their classes taken toward an Associate Degree in order to significantly raise their GPA to above a 3.0. Many colleges offer transfer scholarships to a University. Transfer scholarships are based on your GPA from your Associates Degree classes, not high school grades.

Record the information that you find out on the lines below.

_____

_____

_____

10. It may be too early for you to apply for financial aid through the government, but you can complete the financial aid forecaster anytime. It will give you an estimate of how much financial aid you could qualify for based on your financial situation. You may need an adult's assistance to help you calculate this. The FAFSA4CASTER, can be found at www.YouthWorkbook.com under the Step 5 Resources link.

_____
_____
_____

Note: If you are incarcerated, have a conviction for a drug offense, or are subject to an involuntary civil commitment after completing a period of incarceration for a sexual offense, your eligibility for federal student aid may be limited. Other Basic Eligibility Criteria for Federal Student Aid information that you need to qualify can be found on www.YouthWorkbook.com under the Step 5 Resources link.

Receiving a scholarship or financial aid of any amount will help to reduce how much you have to pay on your own for college. It will also reduce the amount of student loans that you have to take out, if you choose to do so. Talk to your school counselor about other sources of financial support for school.

11. Where will you live while going to school? _____

Will you be responsible for paying any bills where you will be living? _____
If no, then you can skip #12.

12. List the costs for any bills that you will be responsible for in the lines below. Listed are basic utilities that you will need to live comfortably. We did not include luxuries such Wi-Fi and cable, etc. (Tip: If you don't know the average monthly cost for any of the items below, contact the organization listed in the parenthesis to find out the average cost or ask an adult about how much they pay.)

   a. Rent _____ (If you are not sure how much this will be, then you can conduct an apartment search under the Step 5 Resources link on www.YouthWorkbook.com. Be sure to call the apartment to find out if some of the following items are included in the rent, if this information is not already listed on the website.)

   b. Gas_____ (Your local gas company)

   c. Electric_____ (Your local electric company)

   d. Water_____ (Your local water company)

   e. Other_____ (Describe: _____)

13. Do you plan to work? _____

    If yes, then your skills coming directly out of high school will usually qualify you to earn the minimum wage amount per hour in any job. How much is minimum wage currently?
    _____

    If you have another job already lined up which will pay your more than minimum wage, list the amount per hour here. _____

14. How many hours do you plan to work per week once you start school? _____

15. List your ideal school, work, study schedule in the table below. This is to help ensure that you are being realistic with the time you plan to work, study and go to school. Keep in mind that college classes are offered in the morning or evening, usually Monday – Saturday and are usually 2-3 hours long.

	School Time	Work Time	Study Time
Monday			
Tuesday			
Wednesday			
Thursday			
Friday			
Saturday			
Sunday			

16. Calculate how much your gross check amount will be each week. Gross means how much money you make before taxes are taken out of your check. (Hint: Multiply your answer in #14 by how much you will make per hour in #13).
    _____

17. Calculate how much your net check amount will be. This is how much you will actually bring home after the following taxes are taken from your check. The following tax rates are as of 2016:

   a. Multiply the State tax of 4.25% by your answer to #16 and place the amount here: _____

   b. Multiply the Federal tax of 10% by your answer to number #16 and place the amount here: _____

   c. Multiply the FICA tax of 6.2% by your answer to number #16 and place the amount here: _____

   d. Multiply the Medicare tax of 1.45% by your answer to number #16 and place the amount here: _____

   e. Add your answers to a,b,c,d and place the total here: _____

   f. Subtract your answer to "e" above from your answer to #16 and place your answer here: _____. This is your net check amount and is how much you will actually bring home.

18. About how much will the following be each month? You can start trying to figure out how much these will cost by asking an adult about how much they pay for these.
   a. If you will have a car, car insurance cost:_____
   b. If you will have a car note, cost per month:_____
   c. Gas for your car each month:_____
   d. Monthly cell phone bill:_____
   e. Food each month: _____
   f. Bus fare each month, if no car: _____

19. Considering everything that you will have to pay for, will you be able to survive financially on your income? _____

   Why or why not?

   _____
   _____

   Is there anything that you can do to improve your financial situation? Explain.

   _____
   _____

What if...

20. Having some type of emergency savings is always a good idea. If you were to get a flat tire, would you have enough to purchase another tire for $100?

   _____.

If no, what will you do? How will you get it fixed? How will you get to school and work?

_____
_____
_____
_____

Preparing for a job training program

The questionnaire below is helpful for students that plan to attend a job training program.

You will likely not know the answer to many of these questions right away. YouthWorkbook.com is a great resource to help you find answers.

1. What job training program do you plan to attend?

    _____
    _____

    How much is the program?

    _____

2. When do you plan to start school? (Month/Year)_____

3. Are there books or other fees involved in the job training program that you will need to pay for? If yes, list them here:

    _____

4. Depending on your job training program, you may be able to use federal financial aid to help cover the costs of the program. About how much financial aid could you receive? You may need an adult's assistance to help you calculate this. In order to help you figure out how much financial aid you can receive, you can use the FAFSA4CASTER, which can be found at www.YouthWorkbook.com under the Step 5 Resources link.

    _____
    _____
    _____

    Note: If you are incarcerated, have a conviction for a drug offense, or are subject to an involuntary civil commitment after completing a period of incarceration for a sexual offense, your eligibility for federal student aid may be limited. Other things that you need to qualify can be found by doing a Google search for "Basic Eligibility Criteria for Federal Student Aid."

Receiving financial assistance of any amount will help to reduce how much you have to pay on your own for college. It will also reduce the amount of student loans that you have to take out, if you choose to do so. Talk to your school counselor about other sources of financial support for school.

5. Where will you live while going to school? _____

   Will you be responsible for paying any bills where you will be living? _____

6. List the costs for any bills that you will be responsible for in the lines below. Listed are basic utilities that you will need to live comfortably. We did not include luxuries such Wi-Fi and cable, etc. (Tip: If you don't know the average monthly cost for any of the items below, contact the organization listed in the parenthesis to find out the average cost or ask an adult about how much they pay.)

   a. Rent _____ (If you are not sure how much this will be, then you can conduct an apartment search on www.YouthWorkbook.com under the Step 5 Resources link. Be sure to call the apartment to find out if some of the following items are included in the rent, if this information is not already listed on the website.)

   b. Gas_____ (Your local gas company)

   c. Electric_____ (Your local electric company)

   d. Water_____ (Your local water company)

   e. Other_____ (Describe: _____)

7. Do you plan to work? _____

   If yes, then your skills coming directly out of high school will usually qualify you to earn the minimum wage amount per hour in any job. How much is minimum wage? _____

   If you have another job already lined up which will pay your more than minimum wage, list the amount per hour here. _____

   If you already have a job lined up, what is it and how do you know that you will really get it?
   _____
   _____
   _____

8. How many hours do you plan to work per week once you start school? _____

9. List your ideal school, work, study schedule in the table below. This is to help you ensure that you are being realistic with the time you plan to work, study and go to school.

	School Time	Work Time	Study Time
Monday			
Tuesday			
Wednesday			
Thursday			
Friday			
Saturday			
Sunday			

10. Calculate how much your gross check amount will be each week. Gross means how much money you make before taxes are taken out of your check. (Hint: Multiply your answer in #8 by how much you will make per hour in #7)._____

11. Calculate how much your net check amount will be. This is how much you will actual bring home after the following taxes are taken from your check. The following tax rates are as of 2016:

    a. Multiply the State tax of 4.25% by your answer to #10 and place the amount here: _____

    b. Multiply the Federal tax of 10% by your answer to number #10 and place the amount here: _____

    c. Multiply the FICA tax of 6.2% by your answer to number #10 and place the amount here: _____

    d. Multiply the Medicare tax of 1.45% by your answer to number #10 and place the amount here: _____

    e. Add your answers to a,b,c,d and place the total here: _____

    f.   Subtract your answer to "e" from your answer to #10 above and place your answer here: _____. This is your net check amount and is how much you will actually bring home.

12. About how much will the following be each month? You can start trying to figure out how much these will cost by asking an adult about how much they pay for these.
    a.   If you will have a car, car insurance cost:_____
    b.   If you will have a car note, cost per month:_____
    c.   Gas for your car each month:_____
    d.   Monthly cell phone bill:_____
    e.   Food each month: _____
    f.   Bus fare each month, if no car: _____

13. Considering everything that you will have to pay for, will you be able to survive financially on your income? _____

Why or why not?

_____
_____

Is there anything that you can do to improve your financial situation? Explain.

_____
_____

What if…

14. Having some type of emergency savings is always a good idea. If you were to get a flat tire, would you have enough to purchase another tire for $100? _____.

If no, what will you do? How will you get it fixed? How will you get to school and work?

_____
_____

Conclusion

What things do you believe that you can do today so that you are able to succeed in college and not get distracted with the stressors of life as an emerging adult?

_____
_____
_____
_____
_____
_____
_____

What things do you believe that you can do today so that you are becoming more involved in your own education?

_____
_____
_____
_____
_____
_____

What things do you believe that you can do today to keep yourself from getting distracted by negative things that may be going on in your environment either at home, in school or in your community?

_____
_____
_____
_____
_____
_____

What things do you believe that you can do today to increase your self-esteem, become more of a leader and avoid negative peer pressure?

_____
_____
_____
_____
_____
_____

Pretend for a moment that you are a certain type of seed that grows. Use an analogy to explain which type of seed you would like to be and why? Answering this question will require that you do some research on the seed that you chose. (i.e. Some examples of seeds that grow include oranges, raspberries, broccoli, prunes, corn, peaches, mangoes, celery, conifers, tangerines, kiwifruit, gooseberries, plums, pumpkins, beets, starfruit, all types of beans, carrots, asparagus, apples, crabapples, swiss chard, etc.)

_____
_____
_____
_____
_____

Sources:

And Justice for Some. Differential Treatment of Youth of Color in the Justice System (Rep.). (2007, January). Retrieved July 19, 2016, from
http://www.nccdglobal.org/sites/default/files/publication_pdf/justice-for-some.pdf

Centers for Disease Control, Health Risk Behaviors among Adolescents Who Do and Do Not Attend School – United States, 1992, 43 MORBIDITY AND MORTALITY WEEKLY REPORT, Mar. 4, 1994 at 129.

Goertz, M.E., Pollack, J.M. & Rock, D.A. (196). Who drops out of high school and why?: Findings from a national study. Teachers College Record, 87, 357-73, available at www.tcrecord.org/Content.asp?ContentId=688

www.ingramcontent.com/pod-product-compliance
Lightning Source LLC
Chambersburg PA
CBHW081213180526
45170CB00006B/2329